THE
ENDURING
BEAST

THE ENDURING BEAST

edited and illustrated

by Miriam Beerman

1972

Doubleday & Company, Inc.

Garden City, New York

CONTENTS

I. *Animal Nature*

MAY SWENSON	Feel Like a Bird	11
GREGORY CORSO	Giant Turtle	14
ISAK DINESEN	Untitled Poem	17
MARIANNE MOORE	The Wood-Weasel	18
YVOR WINTERS	April	20
EMILY DICKINSON	CIV	23

II. *What Is the World*

EUGENE GUILLEVIC	Dead Titmouse	26
Translated By Denise Levertov		
ROBERT FROST	The Rabbit Hunter	28
ROBERT LOWELL	Mink	30
LEONARD COHEN	Inquiry into the Nature of Cruelty	30
MARGARET ATWOOD	Elegy for the giant tortoises	31
STEPHAN SANDY	from: Midsummer Nights	34
WILLIAM BLAKE	The Fly	36
WILLIAM BUTLER YEATS	To a Squirrel at Kyle-Na-No	38
ROBERT PENN WARREN	from: Was Not the Lost Dauphin	40
DANIEL BERRIGAN	Moment	41

III. Animal Spirit

WALT WHITMAN	from: Song of Myself	44
JOHN MALCOLM BRINNIN	The Giant Turtle Grants an Interview	46
PABLO NERUDA	From: Elephant	48
ELIZABETH BISHOP	Giant Toad	52
DANIEL HOFFMAN	On the Extinction of a Species	54
THEODORE ROETHKE	Snake	55
NED O'GORMAN	The Rhino Stands Still in a Field of Lilies	56
D. H. LAWRENCE	Lizard	59
CARL SANDBURG	Rat Riddles	60
Acknowledgements		62

To Julian, Bill, and my mother

ANIMAL NATURE

Behold Behemoth, which I made as I made you

Job 40:15

FEEL LIKE A BIRD

Feel like a   Bird
Understand
He has no   Hand

Instead a   Wing
Close-lapped
mysterious thing

In sleeveless coat
he halves the   Air
skipping there

like water-licked boat
Lands on   Star-Toes
Finger-beak in

feather-pocket
finds no   Coin
In neat head like   Seeds

in a quartered apple
eyes join
sniping at   Opposites

to stereoscope
the scene before
Close to floor   Giddy

no arms to fling
a   third   Sail
spreads for calm

his tail
Hand better than a   Wing
to gather a   Heap

to count
to clasp a   Mate?
Or   leap

lone-free on muffled
shoulders to span
a   Fate?

Gregory Corso

GIANT TURTLE

from a Walt Disney film

You rise from the sea an agony of sea
Night in the moonlight you slow the shore
Behind you webbed-tracks mark your ordeal
An hour   in an hour you cease your slow
Hind legs now digging   digging the sand the damp the sand
The moon brightens   the sea calms
Your mouth pumping   your eyes thickly tearing
You create a tremendous hole   you fall flat
Exhaust   sigh   strain
Eggs   eggs   eggs   eggs   eggs   eggs   eggs   eggs   eggs
Eggs   eggs   eggs   eggs   egg   egg   egg
Heave   exhaust   sigh   flat
Your wet womb speckled with sand   you turn slow
Slow you cover the hole the eggs slow   slow
You cease your slow
Dawn
And you plop in the sea like a big rock

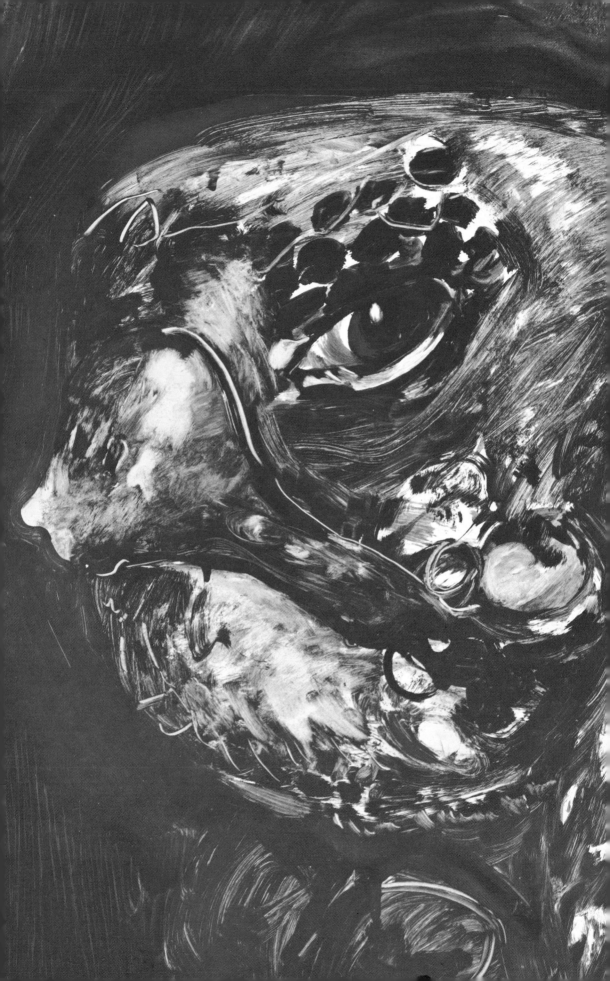

Isak Dinesen

The eagle's shadow runs across the plain,
Towards the distant, nameless, air-blue mountains.
But the shadows of the round young Zebra
Sit close between their delicate hoofs all day,
    where they stand immovable,
And wait for the evening, wait to stretch out, blue,
Upon a plain, painted brick-red by the sunset,
And to wander to the water-hole.

Marianne Moore

THE WOOD-WEASEL

emerges daintily, the skunk—
don't laugh—in sylvan black and white chipmunk
regalia. The inky thing
adaptively whited with glistening
goat-fur, is wood-warden. In his
ermined well-cuttlefish-inked wool, he is
determination's totem. Out-
lawed? His sweet face and powerful feet go about
in chieftain's coat of Chilcat cloth.
He is his own protection from the moth,

noble little warrior. That
otter-skin on it, the living pole-cat,
smothers anything that stings. Well,—
this same weasel's playful and his weasel
associates are too. Only
Wood-weasels shall associate with me.

Yvor Winters

APRIL

The little goat
crops
new grass lying down
leaps up eight inches
into air and
lands on four feet.
Not a tremor—
solid in the
spring and serious
he walks away.

Emily Dickinson

CIV

The bat is dun with wrinkled wings
   Like fallow article,
And not a song pervades his lips,
   Or none perceptible.

His small umbrella, quaintly halved,
   Describing in the air
An arc alike inscrutable,—
   Elate philosopher!

Deputed from what firmament
   Of what astute abode,
Empowered with what malevolence
   Auspiciously withheld.

To his adroit Creator
   Ascribe no less the praise;
Beneficent, believe me,
   His eccentricities.

WHAT IS THE WORLD

He does wrong . . . who shoots birds, hunts animals, digs up the larvae of insects, frightens nesting birds, stops up burrows, carries off nests, wounds pregnant animals , . . does not permit man and beast to rest.

Commandments of the Kan-Ying-P'ien

Eugene Guillevic

translated by Denise Levertov

DEAD TITMOUSE

Is there still talk of thee,
somewhere,
among thy kinsfolk?

Is thy name
still spoken?

Robert Frost

THE RABBIT HUNTER

Careless and still
The hunter lurks
With gun depressed,
Facing alone
The alder swamps
Ghastly snow-white.
And his hound works
In the offing there
Like one possessed,
And yelps delight
And sings and romps,
Bringing him on
The shadowy hare
For him to rend
And deal a death
That he nor it
(Nor I) have wit
To comprehend.

Robert Lowell

MINK

In the unspoiled age, when they caught a cow-mink,
they made her urinate around the traps,
and every bull-mink hunting along the stream
fell in the trap, and soon the mink were done—
the last we heard of was a freeze in the 50's,
the last bull making tracks in the snow for a last cow.
My friend, once professional, no longer traps:
"We've too many ways to make a living now"—
his a veteran's pension, and two working sons.
He builds houses for bluebirds, martins and swallows.
When a pair mates in one, it's like a catch,
like trapping something—he's sent, it's like a conversion,
China's lost will to excel without improving. . . .
His money goes to *Wildlife;* he killed too much.

Leonard Cohen

INQUIRY INTO THE NATURE OF CRUELTY

A moth drowned in my urine,
his powdered body finally satin.
My eyes gleamed in the porcelain
like tiny dancing crematoria.

History is on my side, I pleaded,
as the drain drew circles in his wings.
(Had he not been bathed in urine
I'd have rescued him to dry in the wind.)

Margaret Atwood

ELEGY FOR THE GIANT TORTOISES

Let others pray for the passenger pigeon
the dodo, the whooping crane, the eskimo:
everyone must specialize

I will confine myself to a meditation
upon the giant tortoises
withering finally on a remote island.

I concentrate in subway stations,
in parks, I can't quite see them,
they move to the peripheries of my eyes

but on the last day they will be there;
already the event
like a wave travelling shapes vision:

on the road where I stand they will materialize,
plodding past me in a straggling line
awkward without water

their small heads pondering
from side to side, their useless armour
sadder than tanks and history,

in their closed gaze ocean and sunlight paralysed,
lumbering up the steps, under the archways
toward the square glass altars

where the brittle gods are kept,
the relics of what we have destroyed,
our holy and obsolete symbols.

Stephan Sandy

---

from: MIDSUMMER NIGHTS

From an unpaved road a deer leaps up
foaming in terror to escape
mounting my hood, the windshield, me;
splashing the pane through which I see.

William Blake

THE FLY

LITTLE Fly
Thy summer's play,
My thoughtless hand
Has brush'd away.

Am not I
A fly like thee?
Or art not thou
A man like me?

For I dance
And drink and sing:
Till some blind hand
Shall brush my wing.

If thought is life
And strength and breath:
And the want
Of thought is death;

Then am I
A happy fly,
If I live,
Or if I die.

William Butler Yeats

TO A SQUIRREL AT KYLE-NA-NO

Come play with me;
Why should you run
Through the shaking tree
As though I'd a gun
To strike you dead?
When all I would do
Is to scratch your head
And let you go.

Robert Penn Warren

from: WAS NOT THE LOST DAUPHIN

October: and the bear,
Daft in the honey-light, yawns.

The bear's tongue, pink as a baby's, out-crisps to the curled tip,
It bleeds the black blood of the blueberry.

The teeth are more importantly white
Than has ever been imagined.

The bear feels his own fat
Sweeten, like a drowse, deep to the bone.

Bemused, above the fume of ruined blueberries,
The last bee hums.

The wings, like mica, glint
In the sunlight.

He leans on his gun. Thinks
How thin is the membrane between himself and the world.

Daniel Berrigan

MOMENT

Is the world then, more
than an animal haunch, cleft
under the butcher's ax,
a world hung raw, flayed on a hook?

Is the world more? is it
five or six deer together, standing in dusk
abstract, momentary; then startled, dissolved in
newer and newer rhythms, mauve hoofs, red nostrils
eyes unwary as first stars?

Are we, the watchers
bathed in that sight, a baptism?
The world
for all its stern exactions, loved us once:

homeward in dark, pondering *what is the world?*

ANIMAL SPIRIT

And think how the nightingale, who is so shy,
makes of himself a belfry of throbbing sound . . .

D. H. Lawrence

Walt Whitman

---

from: SONG OF MYSELF

I think I could turn and live with animals, they are so placid and
    self-contain'd,
I stand and look at them long and long.

They do not sweat and whine about their condition,
They do not lie awake in the dark and weep for their sins,
They do not make me sick discussing their duty to God,
Not one is dissatisfied, not one is demented with the mania of
    owning things,
Not one kneels to another, nor to his kind that lived thousands of
    years ago,
Not one is respectable or unhappy over the whole earth.

John Malcolm Brinnin

THE GIANT TURTLE GRANTS AN INTERVIEW

How old are you, Old Silence?
  I tell time that it is.
And are you full of wonder?
  Ephemeral verities.
What most do you long for?
  No end to my retreat.
Have you affections, loves?
  I savor what I eat.
Do shellbacks talk to shells?
  Sea is a single word.
Have you some end in mind?
  No end, and no reward.
Does enterprise command you?
  I manage a good freight.
Has any counsel touched you?
  Lie low. Keep quiet. Wait.
Your days—they have a pattern?
  In the degree of night.
Has solitude a heart?
  If a circle has a center.
Do creatures covet yours?
  They knock, but seldom enter.
Have you not once perceived
  The whole wide world is yours?
I have. Excuse me, I
  Stay utterly indoors.

Pablo Neruda

From: ELEPHANT

Gross innocent,
Saint Elephant,
blessed beast
of the perduring forests,
bulk of our palpable world
in its counterpoise,
mighty
and exquisite,
a saddlery's cosmos
in leather,
ivory
packed into satins
unmoved
like
the flesh of the moon,
minimal eyes
to observe, without being observed,
horn
virtuoso
and bugling.
propinquity,
animal
waterspout
elate
in
its
cleanliness,
portable
engine
and telephone booth in a forest:
so
softly you go
in your swagger,
with your aging caparison
in the wrinkle and pile
of a tree's regimentals,
your pants
at your ankles,
trailing your tail-end.

Make no mistake:
that endeared and enormous
sojourner of jungles is nobody's clown;
he is patriarch,
father of emerald lights,
the ancient
and innocent
sire of the universe.

All the fruits of the earth,
and the longings
of Tantalus,
the multitudinous
skin
and the ways of

the rain
have encompassed
the kingdom of
elephants;
with brine
and
with blood
they accomplished the war
of their species in silence.

The scale-bearing kind,
the lizards-turned-lion,
the fish in the mountains
and gargantuan ground sloth
succumbed
and decayed:
they
leavened the green of the bog,
a prize
for the sweltering fly
and the scarab's barbarity.
But the elephant rose
on the wreck of his fears—
almost a vegetable, a shadowy pylon
in his emerald heaven,
to suckle his young
on the sweet of the leaves, and the water
and honey of stones. . . .

GIANT TOAD

I am too big, too big by far. Pity me.

My eyes bulge and hurt. They are my one great beauty, even so. They see too much, above, below, and yet there is not much to see. The rain has stopped. The mist is gathering on my skin in drops. The drops run down my back, run from the corners of my downturned mouth, run down my sides and drip beneath my belly. Perhaps the droplets on my mottled hide are pretty, like dewdrops, silver on a moldering leaf? They chill me through and through. I feel my colors changing now, my pigments gradually shudder and shift over.

Now I shall get beneath that overhanging ledge. Slowly. Hop. Two or three times more, silently. That was too far. I'm standing up. The lichen's gray, and rough to my front feet. Get down. Turn facing out, it's safer. Don't breathe until the snail gets by. But we go travelling the same weathers.

Swallow the air and mouthfuls of cold mist. Give voice, just once. O how it echoed from the rock! What a profound, angelic bell I rang!

I live, I breathe, by swallowing. Once, some naughty children picked me up, me and two brothers. They set us down again somewhere and in our mouths they put lit cigarettes. We could not help but smoke them, to the end. I thought it was the death of me, but when I was entirely filled with smoke, when my slack mouth was burning, and all my tripes were hot and dry, they let us go. But I was sick for days.

I have big shoulders, like a boxer. They are not muscle, however, and their color is dark. They are my sacs of poison, the almost unused poison that I bear, my burden and my great responsibility. Big wings of poison, folded on my back. Beware, I am an angel in disguise; my wings are evil, but not deadly. If I will it, the poison could break through, blue-black, and dangerous to all. Blue-black fumes would rise upon the air. Beware, you frivolous crab.

Daniel Hoffman

ON THE EXTINCTION
OF A SPECIES

Avast, the Pileated Woodpecker:
Square-hole-knocker in the pine,
Wears his ivory tower as hatchetnose
Crested with a wedge of flame,
& busily bangs his wooden signature.

Death drops more birds than birds drop eggs
—Promethean feathers on suburban hills
Are rare. But those square holes
[Dark images] in a living frame
Endure , endure , endure , endure.

Theodore Roethke

SNAKE

I saw a young snake glide
Out of the mottled shade
And hang, limp on a stone:
A thin mouth, and a tongue
Stayed, in the still air.

It turned; it drew away;
Its shadow bent in half;
It quickened, and was gone.

I felt my slow blood warm.
I longed to be that thing,
The pure, sensuous form.

And I may be, some time.

Ned O'Gorman

THE RHINO STANDS STILL
IN A FIELD OF LILIES

His eyes
two points
of damage
in the
breast of
a cut
down giant:
his legs
four axies
of planet
Mars: his
neck the
barrel of
a still
cannon: his
ears two
gates of
Tophet: his
belly is
a drum
of lead
over a
drum of
copper over
a drum
of black
bone: his
paws: four
bolts: his
mouth the
slit back
of a
scarab: the

rhino stands
still as
a balanced
rock over
a wedding
march: as
a deaf
nun on
a cymbal.

The difference
between man
and rhino
is that
when the
lilies moved
on their
stems I
looked down
and it
did not:
when the
black crane
cooed on
the pitch
of the
snow face
I covered
my eyes
and picked
up a
stone: it
did not.

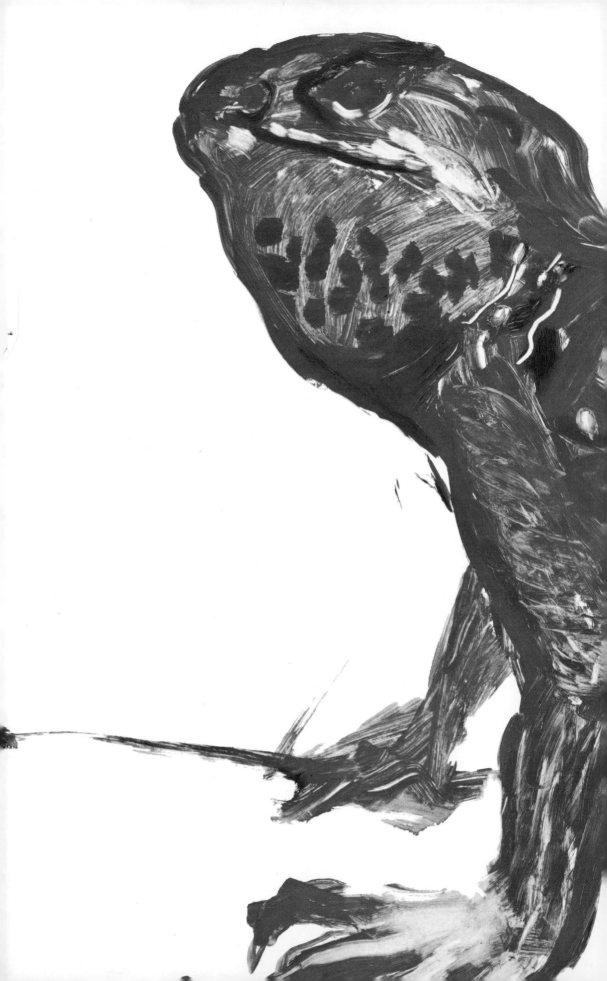

D. H. Lawrence

LIZARD

A lizard ran out on a rock and looked up, listening
no doubt to the sounding of the spheres.
And what a dandy fellow! the right toss of a chin for you
and swirl of a tail!

If men were as much men as lizards are lizards
they'd be worth looking at.

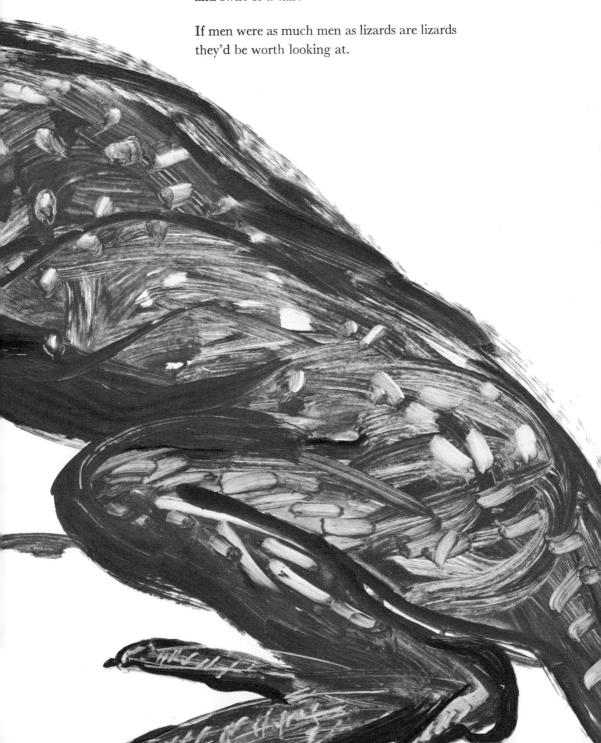

Carl Sandburg

RAT RIDDLES

THERE was a gray rat looked at me
with green eyes out of a rathole.

"Hello, rat," I said,
"Is there any chance for me
to get on to the language of the rats?"

And the green eyes blinked at me,
blinked from a gray rat's rathole.

"Come again," I said,
"Slip me a couple of riddles;
there must be riddles among the rats."

And the green eyes blinked at me
and a whisper came from the gray rathole:
"Who do you think you are and why is a rat?
  Where did you sleep last night and why do
    you sneeze on Tuesdays? And why is the
    grave of a rat no deeper than the grave
    of a man?"

And the tail of a green-eyed rat
Whipped and was gone at a gray rathole.

ACKNOWLEDGEMENTS

Grateful acknowledgment is made to the following publishers and individuals for permission to use poems under their control:

Atlantic-Little, Brown and Co. for "Elegy for the giant tortoises" from *The Animals in that Country* by Margaret Atwood. Copyright © 1968 by Oxford University Press (Canadian Branch); CIV ("The bat is dun with wrinkled wings") from *Poems by Emily Dickinson* edited by Martha Dickinson Bianchi and Arthur Leete Hampson.

The Bodley Head for "The Fly" by William Blake from *William Blake,* edited by J. Bronowski.

John Malcolm Brinnin for "The Giant Turtle Grants an Interview," copyright 1963 by John Malcolm Brinnin. Originally appeared in *The New Yorker.*

Doubleday & Company, Inc. for "Snake" copyright © 1955 by Theodore Roethke from *The Collected Poems of Theodore Roethke;* for lines from "Song of Myself" from *Leaves of Grass* by Walt Whitman.

Farrar, Straus & Giroux, Inc. for "Mink" from *Notebook* by Robert Lowell, copyright © 1967, 1968, 1969, 1970 by Robert Lowell; for "The Giant Toad" from *The Complete Poems* by Elizabeth Bishop, copyright © 1967, 1969 by Elizabeth Bishop.

Grove Press, Inc. for lines from "From: Elephant" from *Selected Poems of Pablo Neruda* edited and translated by Ben Belitt. Copyright © 1961 by Grove Press, Inc., English texts copyright © 1961 by Ben Belitt.

Harcourt, Brace Jovanovich, Inc. for "The Rhino Stands Still in a Field of Lilies," *From 3 African Poems for the Children Shrady* in *The Buzzard and the Peacock,* copyright © 1964 by Ned O'Gorman; "Rat Riddles" from *Good Morning, America,* copyright 1928, 1956 by Carl Sandburg.

Daniel Hoffman for "On the Extinction of a Species" from *An Armada of Thirty Whales,* copyright © 1954 by Yale University Press.

Holt, Rinehart and Winston, Inc. for "The Rabbit Hunter" from *The Poetry of Robert Frost* edited by Edward Connery Lathem; copyright 1942 by Robert Frost, copyright © 1970 by Leslie Frost Ballantine.

Houghton Mifflin Company for lines from "Midsummer Nights" from *Stresses in the Peaceable Kingdom* by Stephan Sandy. Copyright © 1960, 1961, 1962, 1963, 1964, 1965, 1966, 1967 by Stephan Sandy.

MIRIAM BEERMAN is a very talented painter whose work hangs in the permanent collections of the Brooklyn Museum, the Whitney Museum, the Andrew Dickson White Museum at Cornell University, the New School, New York and many private collections. She conducts art workshops for children at Muse (Brooklyn's Children Museum), exhibits at the Graham Gallery, New York, and recently received a grant from the Cultural Council Foundation, a public service program, and she will be having several exhibitions in New York in the future.